Genre Expository Text

Essential Question
How do you explain what you see in the sky?

Stargazing

by Rachel Hayward

Chapter 1

Ancient Views of the Skies

For thousands of years, people have looked up at the night sky and wondered about the stars moving above them. They have tried to map what they have seen in the skies, and they have told stories about the moon and the stars.

The Lascaux *(la-SKOH)* caves in France contain cave paintings made more than 16,000 years ago during the Stone Age. One of the paintings depicts a bird-man standing next to a bull and a bird. Some scientists think that this is a chart of the three stars that make up the Summer Triangle.

Scientists think these images represent patterns of stars in the sky.

The Milky Way looks like a cloudy band of stars in the night sky.

As well as mapping the stars, ancient people created stories about the stars' beginnings. For example, the Shoshone tell an old story that explains how the stars of the Milky Way came to be in the sky.

Once, a grizzly bear decided to go hunting in the sky. He scrambled up a huge, snowy mountain. Ice crystals clung to the bear's thick, shaggy fur.

When he reached the top of the mountain, the bear leaped out into the sky. The ice crystals shook loose and scattered behind him across the sky. The crystals became the stars of the Milky Way.

Earth on the Move

Many ancient people also believed that a dome covered Earth. They thought that the dome had holes and that light shone through the holes as stars.

Later, astronomers believed that the sun and stars revolved around Earth. In Ancient Greece, Plato described this theory. It is easy to understand why when we look at the sky. The sun and stars appear to travel across the sky. However, it's Earth that actually moves.

Imagine that Earth is a basketball. Then imagine that you could push a thin metal pole through the center of the ball. That pole represents Earth's axis. The North Pole is at the top of the axis. The South Pole is at the bottom.

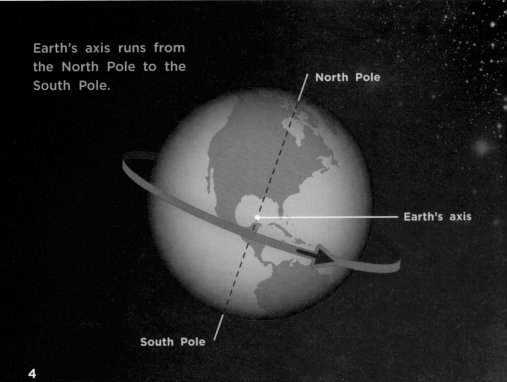

Earth's axis runs from the North Pole to the South Pole.

North Pole

Earth's axis

South Pole

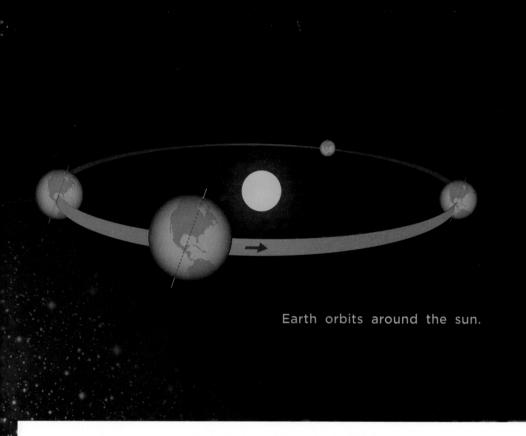

Earth orbits around the sun.

Earth rotates, or turns, around its axis. It makes one complete turn each day (24 hours). We are so small that we don't feel Earth rotating.

At the same time that Earth rotates on its axis, it also **orbits** the sun. It takes one year (365 days) for Earth to make a complete trip around the sun.

Imagine you are spinning the Earth basketball on your fingertip. Each spin is one day. Now imagine that the basketball hoop is the sun. Walk around the basketball hoop with the Earth basketball still spinning on your fingertip. One complete lap around the basketball hoop represents one year.

Chapter 2

Sky Maps
and Calendars

Although people from ancient times didn't understand how Earth moved, they became skilled at mapping the stars and using different stars to navigate.

A Guiding Star

When traveling on land, you can use landmarks such as mountains and rivers to navigate. However, there are no landmarks when you're on the open ocean. The Vikings often sailed close to land so they could use landmarks to find their way. Other sailors went farther out. They used the series of things they saw in the sky to navigate. They used "skymarks" instead of landmarks!

The rising and setting sun showed east and west during the daytime. The position of the stars helped sailors navigate at night.

One star is a very useful guide. For centuries, people have noticed that the North Star, or polestar, doesn't appear to move in the night sky.

Sailors used maps and the stars to navigate across the ocean at night.

The North Star sits almost directly above the northern end of Earth's axis. This is why it doesn't appear to move. Earth rotates, but its axis doesn't move. It always points to the North Star. Other stars in the sky appear to move around the North Star.

The North Star is part of the group of stars named Ursa Minor, or the Little Dipper. It is useful for navigation because it allows people to find north easily. For thousands of years, sailors have used the North Star to navigate across the oceans.

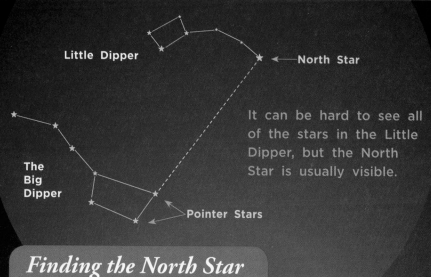

Little Dipper

North Star

The Big Dipper

It can be hard to see all of the stars in the Little Dipper, but the North Star is usually visible.

Pointer Stars

Finding the North Star

The Pointer Stars can help you locate the North Star. You can find them by locating the Big Dipper, the group of stars that looks like a ladle or a scoop. The Pointer Stars are at the right end of the bowl of the Big Dipper. Use an imaginary line to connect them, then extend that line farther, and it will lead you to the North Star. The North Star sits at the end of the Little Dipper's handle.

The Passage of Time

People have also used specific stars to mark the passage of time. Long before they knew that Earth revolved around the sun, people noticed that some stars appear in the night sky at the same time each year. This happens because Earth is moving. As Earth orbits the sun, the part of the night sky that we can see changes.

People made accurate star charts to track these changes. The charts showed the stars' positions in the sky throughout the year.

Stars are grouped into patterns known as **constellations**. It's easier to track a constellation than a single star in the huge night sky. The ancient Greeks identified many constellations and named them after mythological gods and heroes.

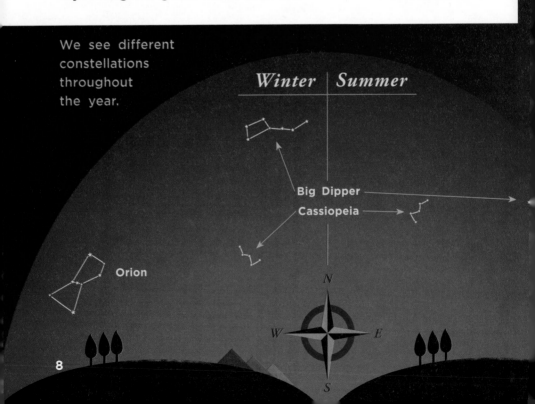

We see different constellations throughout the year.

Winter | Summer

Big Dipper
Cassiopeia
Orion

N
W — E
S

In some cultures, the appearance of certain stars indicated that it was time to plant or harvest their crops. There is a cluster of stars known as the Pleiades *(PLEE-uh-deez)*. People in Hawaii knew it was time to harvest their crops when these stars appeared in the night sky. The Ancient Egyptians knew when the Nile would flood each year based on the location of the star Sirius.

People also used the moon to mark the passage of time. The moon takes almost a month (29.5 days) to orbit Earth. During its orbit, the moon seems to change shape. At first, we see a tiny sliver, then a larger crescent moon, and finally a round full moon. After that, the moon seems to shrink each night until we don't see it at all. Then the cycle repeats. The changing shape of the moon is called the phases of the moon. Many early calendars were based on the phases of the moon.

Chapter 3

Tools for Studying Space

People's fascination with the night skies led them to develop several useful inventions. These inventions revealed more about the stars and space and greatly changed our understanding of the **universe**.

The First Telescope

One of the best tools for looking at the stars is a telescope. In the 1600s, an Italian scientist named Galileo used a telescope to study the moon, stars, and planets.

Galileo was fascinated by **mechanics**. He didn't invent the telescope, but he greatly improved the way it worked. The first telescope appeared in 1608. Early telescopes **magnified** objects to make them look three times closer. By the end of 1609, Galileo had built a powerful telescope that magnified objects so they looked 20 times closer. Galileo's telescope let him see things that no one had seen before.

This telescope is similar to the one used by Galileo.

Galileo's telescope helped him discover that the surface of the moon was covered in mountains and valleys. He counted four moons orbiting the planet Jupiter. He learned that the Milky Way is made up of a huge number of stars.

Jupiter's four largest moons are called the Galilean satellites.

Jupiter

moons

Most importantly, Galileo's studies of the night sky also provided proof that Earth orbited the sun instead of the sun orbiting Earth. His discoveries shocked some people, but they also helped people understand Earth's place in the universe.

Modern Telescopes

Galileo died in 1642, but more than 350 years later, the telescope is still the most useful tool for studying space. Today's telescopes can see far beyond anything Galileo could have imagined.

One of the most important telescopes ever built is the Hubble Space Telescope. This telescope is named after the American astronomer Dr. Edwin Hubble. It floats in space above Earth's atmosphere. This gives us a much clearer view of the stars because we are not looking through Earth's atmosphere.

The atmosphere is the layer of gases that surrounds Earth. The movement of the atmospheric gases **distorts** what we can see through a telescope on Earth. That distortion causes the stars to appear to "twinkle." Earth's atmosphere is also full of dust, which makes it difficult to see things in space.

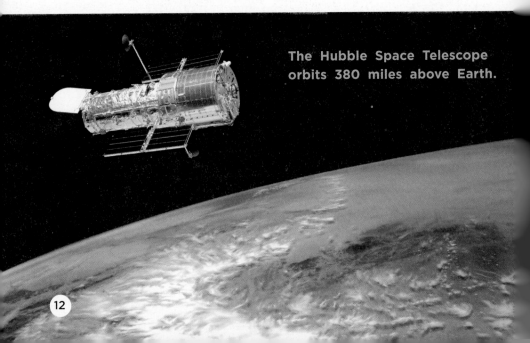

The Hubble Space Telescope orbits 380 miles above Earth.

The Hubble telescope has sent more than 570,000 pictures to Earth. About 4,000 astronomers have used information from Hubble's images to help them answer important questions.

The telescope has helped scientists discover the existence of new **galaxies**. It has shown how galaxies form. It has also helped scientists figure out the age of the universe. Scientists now believe that the universe is about 13 to 14 billion years old.

This is an image of Saturn taken by the Hubble Space Telescope.

(bkgd) Stocktrek Images/Getty Images, (inset) NASA, ESA, J. Clarke (Boston University) and Z. Levay (STScI)

The Hubble Space Telescope

The Hubble telescope is almost 44 feet long and about 14 feet across at its widest point. It travels at a speed of about 5 miles per second and orbits Earth once every 97 minutes. The telescope was put into orbit in 1990 by the *Discovery* space shuttle.

There are plans to replace the Hubble with a bigger telescope named the James Webb Space Telescope. The Webb telescope will sit in space more than a million miles away from Earth, and it will help astronomers to see even farther into space. It will use **infrared vision** to discover objects in space, such as new galaxies and stars.

There are still many things to discover about our universe. Just like the people who lived thousands of years ago, we continue to stare up at the stars and wonder.

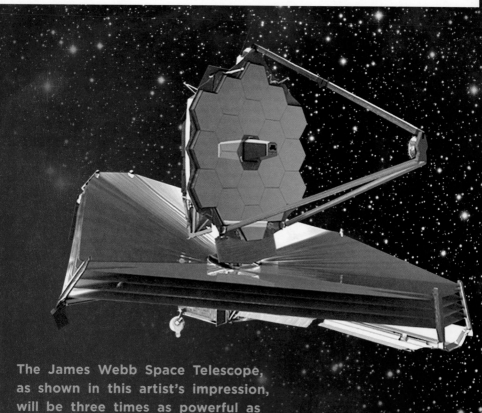

The James Webb Space Telescope, as shown in this artist's impression, will be three times as powerful as the Hubble.

Respond to Reading

Summarize

Use the most important details from *Stargazing* to summarize the selection. Your graphic organizer may help.

Cause → Effect
→
→
→
→

Text Evidence

1. What text features of expository nonfiction do you find in *Stargazing?* How do they help you understand the text better? **GENRE**

2. Why do some constellations only appear at certain times of the year? **CAUSE AND EFFECT**

3. What does *navigate* mean in the second paragraph on page 6? Which context clues helped you figure out the meaning? **PARAGRAPH CLUES**

4. Write about the effects of Galileo's improvements to the telescope. What did people learn about the universe? Use details from the text in your answer. **WRITE ABOUT READING**

Compare Texts

Read about how the constellation Orion
was created.

ORION THE HUNTER

There once lived a man named Orion. His father was
the great sea god, Poseidon. Orion was so strong that he
could carry a whole tree on his shoulders.

Orion was good at many things, but he was especially
skilled at hunting. He hunted with a sword and a club
and carried a shield to protect himself. Orion's two
hunting dogs went with Orion everywhere.

One day, Orion traveled to the island of Crete, where
Artemis lived. She was a great hunter, just like Orion.
Artemis was tall and strong. She hunted with a bow and
arrow, and no one could match her skill at hunting.

When Artemis met Orion, she realized that she had
finally met a hunter who was as skilled as she. Before
long, they hunted together, and they became good friends.

Artemis had a brother named Apollo. Apollo had always been Artemis's best friend. He became very jealous when he saw how much Artemis enjoyed Orion's friendship.

At last, Apollo came up with a plan to end Orion's friendship with his sister. He hid a scorpion in some sand where he knew Orion would walk.

Soon Orion wandered along the path looking for Artemis. His bare foot landed on the scorpion. The scorpion lashed out with its tail and stung Orion on the heel. Even a strong man like Orion was no match for a scorpion's poison. Orion fell to the ground and died.

Artemis was brokenhearted. She called on the gods to place Orion in the sky among the stars with his faithful dogs beside him. The gods agreed to do as she asked.

Today you can still see Orion in the night sky with his belt of three bright stars. You might also see the stars that make up the shape of the scorpion.

The scorpion and Orion are never together in the same part of the sky, however. Orion's stars disappear over the horizon when the scorpion's stars rise. Orion has learned the hard way that he must watch out for the scorpion's sting!

CRETE

Make Connections

Why did Artemis ask the gods to place Orion in the sky? ESSENTIAL QUESTION

Compare the Shoshone explanation of the Milky Way in *Stargazing* with the myth *Orion the Hunter*. Why did people tell stories like these? TEXT TO TEXT

Glossary

constellations *(kon-stuh-LAY-shuhnz)* groups of stars that form patterns *(page 8)*

distorts *(dis-TAWRTS)* changes or alters *(page 12)*

galaxies *(GA-luhk-seez)* large groups of stars in the universe *(page 13)*

infrared vision *(in-fruh-RED VIZH-uhn)* the ability to detect heat waves from the invisible part of the light spectrum *(page 14)*

magnified *(MAG-nuh-fighd)* made to look bigger *(page 10)*

mechanics *(muh-KAN-iks)* the way things move and work *(page 10)*

orbits *(AWR-bits)* moves in a circular path in space *(page 5)*

universe *(YEW-nuh-vurs)* everything that is in existence, from everything on and including Earth to all the planets, stars, and objects in space *(page 10)*

Index

Focus on Science

Purpose To describe what you see in the night sky

Procedure

Step 1 Research constellations using the library or the Internet. Select a constellation that is easy to see in your night sky.

Step 2 Make a labeled diagram of the constellation, naming as many features as you can. Use scientific information from your research to help describe the constellation.

Step 3 Now write a fictional story. You should write your own version of how the constellation formed. Use what you know about myths and legends to help you.

Step 4 Ask your classmates to compare the scientific and fictional descriptions. Which will best help them find the constellation at night?

Conclusion How did making your diagram connect to what you read in *Stargazing*? How was your story similar to or different from other myths and legends you know about constellations?